**milk & other poems**

Also by Rory Harris
*over the outrow*
*from the residence*
*snapshots from a moving train*
*16 poems*
*uncle Jack and other poems*
*waterline*
*breeze*
*songs*
*beach*
*skin*

**Rory Harris**

# milk & other poems

for Hazel

*milk* & *other poems*
ISBN 978 1 76109 327 2
Copyright © text Rory Harris 2022
Cover image: linocut by Hazel Harris, *Friends*, 2013

First published 2022 by
**Ginninderra Press**
PO Box 3461 Port Adelaide 5015
www.ginninderrapress.com.au

# Contents

| | |
|---|---|
| where | 9 |
| change | 10 |
| wire | 11 |
| dance | 12 |
| cast | 13 |
| flight | 14 |
| light | 15 |
| pattern | 17 |
| line | 18 |
| hold | 19 |
| earth | 20 |
| mother | 21 |
| eyes | 22 |
| salt | 23 |
| smoke | 24 |
| lunch | 25 |
| colour | 27 |
| crack | 28 |
| for Tate | 29 |
| duty | 30 |
| touch | 31 |
| tear | 32 |
| sowing | 33 |
| cooks | 34 |
| after | 36 |
| far | 37 |
| small deaths | 38 |
| wonder | 39 |
| drink | 40 |
| bird | 41 |

| | |
|---|---|
| sand | 61 |
| café | 62 |
| change | 63 |
| south | 64 |
| hand | 65 |
| north daughter | 66 |
| August | 70 |
| camel rides | 71 |
| return | 72 |
| hospice | 73 |
| between | 74 |
| bud | 75 |
| suns | 76 |
| ghosts | 78 |
| wrap | 80 |
| green | 81 |
| air | 82 |
| pose | 83 |
| away | 84 |
| shake | 85 |
| blue line | 86 |
| for Florence | 87 |
| wishing | 88 |
| the father | 89 |
| patterns | 90 |
| grief | 91 |
| note | 99 |
| tears | 100 |
| for Reginald Whitely cfc | 104 |
| against | 105 |
| take | 106 |
| cloak | 107 |

| | |
|---|---|
| junk | 108 |
| story | 109 |
| daughter, Chinatown | 110 |
| body | 111 |
| roots | 112 |
| reach | 113 |
| Mila | 114 |
| ward | 115 |
| before | 117 |
| pier | 118 |
| milk | 119 |
| old roads | 120 |
| shape | 121 |
| cold | 122 |
| wait | 123 |
| blue | 124 |
| steam | 125 |
| view | 127 |
| Dorset suite | 128 |
| & now | 132 |
| there | 133 |
| wide | 134 |
| touch | 135 |
| cemetery | 136 |
| caught | 137 |
| slide | 139 |
| | |
| Acknowledgements | 140 |

## **where**

& where to take
these histories
in the gifts of food
& time, patting down
an old man's bed
a wisdom that is not
wise any more
my daughters fold
over the corners
of the page
to mark the place
they are up to
& return to pick
up the story
there is more than
one story
but there is only
one that counts
& I tell it
to my children
I turn back the covers
of my father's bed
& I have done this
many times before

## change

Heavy grey out
of season thick coat

summer hanging
over the beach

a sandal marooned
on the incoming tide

**wire**

A rattle
of sun

through
the blinds

as a razor
would divide

the day
with wire

## dance

The plastic
bag twists

in the breeze
as breath

would keep it
dancing limbs

of a child
the first trusted

step on an earth
firm & anxious

for this & the next
& the one after that

**cast**

The hide

& seek sun

on a thread

cast-off

from the end

of the jetty

## flight

The gulls lift up like hands
these fingers of rain
as feathers once filled pillows

## light

A rattling
of children

through you
front of

the house
screen door

swings, the wire
punctured with

a generation
of finger

holes poked
& mended

& re-poked
until a moment

of grace
a lifting

of shoulders
for the patterns

arranged on
the hallway

floor when
light

catches
as unskilled

emotions would
calm a just-born child

**pattern**

In my father's
late afternoon

a few drinks
under the belt

order of things
the Sunday roast

browns & the sun
yes, the sun

waits on the horizon

## line

Flat line horizon
a string pulled tight
so in the fading
rippling of you
this day sets
as a child would
slam a door

## hold

In the gathering
up of you

a day spread
across a creased brow

as string would
hold you for

an instant
before the first break

the knotted ends
wave in breath

letting a tide
come in

letting a tide
go out

## earth

& the light
in that hour

or so before
the sun drops

& stick
figures walk

a line where
sand & sea

quiver & roll
as I have

drawn you
from memory

& still taste
salt & hear

your heart beat
against the earth

## mother

Her arms
are always

spread as
if flight

would lift
her, but

for a child
at each hand

**eyes**

A curl lip wave breaks
the sun in the corner
flat & wide & white

take it, hang it, over
your thin freckled shoulders
into your green eyes

**salt**

As a hand
has held

you quivering
as emptiness

would turn
a day

into the blue
black unfashioned

dye missing
a beat of time

when streaks
of sun are thrown

across the bay
& the foreshore

cackles a carnival
& twilight

grease fills
a childhood of salt

## smoke

Cold wrap
pink-tipped

ears, a gag
of muffler

to keep
the steam

of words
from smoking

in the new light

## lunch

It's difficult
to look him
in the eyes
hunched over
a bowl of soup
a dressing gown
given up to the day
extensions sewn to
to lengthen
his pyjama pants
rags tucked under
his pillow
his side of the bed
I have pulled tight
& just made it
as a son would
find a little comfort
the made bed
exotic food bought
& packed in
the refrigerator
a quick sweep through
the house
& the straightening
of furniture
heavy featured
like his face
over the soup

the stewing pan
in the sink
filled, tepid
with water
tepid with tears
a rattle of a spoon
in a single bowl

## colour

& you call me in
to examine the blood
in the toilet
& there floating
among your stools
are these clotted
universes, tendrils
swirl to turn
the water pink
your body passes
blood, your one
kidney excretes
urine fuelled
by the alcohol
you drink
in the twilight
cocktail hour
of the day
just before
the sun would
streak the Gulf
& turn the water
a pink wash
at our wounded feet

## crack

& when you have
had enough
to drink
this house
of cards
the crack
in the wall
from a 1954 tremor
I believe I felt
in the crib
as you gathered
me up all those
years ago
& took me to
your bedroom
I sit opposite
you, in the age
it takes to shatter
a trembling hand
a drinking glass
a history of shards

## for Tate

& it was
your broad shoulders
which stopped
your coming
wholly forth
into the new light
caught between
this &
other worlds
your eyes closed
to any coercion
your head appearing
& then a panic
of minutes
& stay while
madness fraught
o small child
heartbeat upon
missing heartbeat
your parents
rattling life
for this one
& for the next
& for the one
after that

## **duty**

Three sheets to the wind
you phone to describe
a father's love
his almost love
& in the absence of love
what love would look like
rattling around
your laminex kitchen
fifty years & two changes of lino
& the adhesive pictures of fruit
my mother stuck on tiles
around the stove
to make it modern
brass hinges on painted cupboards
that you complained about but screwed
your drink is within reach
of the past, of ghosts
floating & feeding themselves
if not on love, then duty
if not on duty, then guilt
a slurp of mouthpiece
a call heavy & handled less well
than it should have been

## touch

These fingers comb down
your eyes to flutter you to sleep

a few strands of hair
waved back a brush of hand

arm in arm a link of elbows
dragging the night across your eyes

you hug me from behind
a quick rattle of a question

there is only yes
there is always only yes

**tear**

Your hands
plunged dug

deep into
blue pockets

a wool
collar pulled

more against
the weather

than fashion
the line

of your
shoulders bends

your hair
in streams

set alight
in the wind

& a warm rain
on your cheeks

past blinking
past care

**sowing**

& finally
a rattling

rain bringing
down the tone

a fluttering
fingers of leaves

a little green
through the dust

as palms
of children

would turn
& cup & later

dance, planting
new seed

scaring the birds
back into the sky

## cooks

From behind
the quiet

rolling waves
your eyes

stare out
further than

the middle
distance

where the television
more sound

than image
sits in late

Saturday
forget the sports

afternoon
your un-Australian

activity more
mine than

your blindness
this revolution

without sight
can change heart

in the holding
of hands

in the soft
food feeding

a miracle of care
& if a country

surrounded
by water

could employ
enough cooks

imagine the feast
for the neighbours

brown long necks
of grace

a plate full of potatoes
& soft cooked meats

which could
feed the old

& the young
& the toothless

before & after
a moment's liberation

## after

The afternoon shadows
stretch long & even

into a crow's feet
squint along that line

where the sea ends
& the broad quick stroke

blue the last colour
from a child's paint

tin sweeps up
a yellow sun

already in the top
right hand corner

& the final piece
still wet but held up

anyway under the chin
maybe this happened

the fourth day

**far**

In that far
away look

way past
where your

eyes would
rest, a thin

blue line
horizon

a little mist
blurring big

as a hand
almost out

of control
sky that even

on your best
days can't

be held up
with your dreaming

there in the salt
smear air, on the beach

your face in the wind
staring out to sea

## small deaths

The shape
of you

as air
would strike

us stepping
into the day

our arms
around your

magnitude
your tiny death

swaddling birth
as perhaps

as on your
anniversary

we remember
to breathe

## wonder

There inside this growing wonder
you protect yourself

walking widely around the furniture
hands below the crescent moon

## drink

Before the first drink of the day
my mother would walk her garden
bend & pull a few weeds
rattle a box of matches & strike a cigarette
more habit than larrikin
stuck at a Digger angle
& continue her bending & smoking
until the four o'clock sun is caught
in the apricot tree over the kitchen window
& return inside to pour
two good fingers & a little soda water
strike a fresh cigarette
then after the slap of plates & cutlery
two more drinks
before the chops are grilled

## bird

Flight as birds

shopping mall dreaming

hotel room, smoking on the street
the taxicab smile negotiate distance
a tape measure of quotes

brand name icons blush in neon

the brilliance of green
chocolate-box orchids
row upon row

elephants perform
a choreography of movements

in a town built on reclaimed land
a gift from a neighbour

& the hint of lizard air

& then road circus
hit me if you can dreaming

dealing in the night time
hum humid

& watch daughters merge with the traffic

hotel small air con haven & *why
weren't we here 20 years ago?*

*but there was other stuff to do*
there is always other stuff

fresh fruit, a little salt & chilli
having left the backpack in the middle from youth

walking the walk around the park square

the breakfast stalls throw open their pots

Notre Dame Cathedral
*No go through mass is being*
lighting a candle or two
postcards & prayer
a long shave in candle light
a head massage power failure

children selling Kerouac's *On the Road*
with Zadie Smith
the rolling wind throws down the rain
cramped at the entrance of the hotel drinking

a country which exercises so well
in the morning
& smokes so heavily at night
just has to be grand

& I won't even mention
how good the food is

at the tourist office
the common language of parents
our children & school fees

later we sit as family
dusting off the day

jumping from taxi to footpath
patchworked as we go shop to shop
in the overcast afternoon

hawkers fly on the wing
& somehow survive

the small child sleeps
curled around cardboard
a sibling's open palm

what is the exchange rate for a single US dollar?
forget that it's an election year

where of the giving & grace
of postcards as we rest
under the verandas from afternoon rain

stories sing like the overhead wires
until a tree falls then there is a little thinking to do

green coconut dreaming

here we hang our hats
for the stretch of days
our heads & our hearts are full

I light a candle for Lucas's father
*I'll teach you more in death than in life*
we both agree it's a good line
I make sure the candle is firm

beardless my fresh cheeks in the rain

the days flash by in the damp
rolling air, a little grace
& the money exchange

the wires wave along the street
freeways of electricity
somehow it all gets through

windmills of arms in the cool
& bodies bend a little
in the new light sun high up

through lanes of antiques
porcelain & brass going way back

the sound of two hands clapping
to get rid of a single sparrow
in a department store
all this walking the morning mill

old traveller backpack along gossip track

frayed in the damp my collar sticks
the night is glue gun thick

Memorial Cultural Park
the swaying leaves
as hips work their way through
the morning air exercised

gestures turned into art forms
a borrowed piece of wood from a cyclo driver
to sit on outside the shop

the short jump start heart into Cambodia

frangipani line the streets
pink bud white bud
three copies of Karl Skinner's *Walden Two*
in a Phnom Penh Bookshop for $2.50 US a piece

torture was the explicit curriculum
here there is only grief

laid bare weeping sore heart break
a flock of black birds through our liberation

puddles of blood puddles of tears
having sat on our hands not listening to the weeping
as rain would fill our hearts

frangipani does not rattle its petals
their brittle stems our veins

there are shores to swim towards
& there are shores to leave behind
what makes an island is the swim around it

water brushes over white stone
no snow, in the gecko filled night

heavy & slow this history around us like a string

the wooden houses stacked & tacked
nailed like the boxed ends of crates
there are no dripping louvers here

my oldest daughter carries the umbrella
drops arc around her

sitting Buddha over espressos

the hotel has a shrine, a pool
smells of cigarettes
& not a grilled lamb chop anywhere

the buildings throw up
their shape in the dust

where a few miles away
ancient Gods shuffle
their heavy history

always the morning
straw broom over tiles
wet feet glide as a childhood of grazes

a mobile phone plays junk

the even rhythm
scratch of sweeping
as the hotel generator hums its mantra

in the breakfast light
the gods rattle their cutlery

next door the school
sings the morning

in the dirty tropic this movement
families gather in all forms
as limbs would fall from bodies

a few hours after the cock crow dawn I rattle a cigarette
while my daughters turn into fish
swimming laps in the hotel's pool

murder spills over a postage stamp

the overhead fan works overtime in the afternoon's heat

wind over us
as the dust collects
in the pockets of the room

loose change
tips from the ruling class

litter turns to mush
paper boats sail & rivers flow

of lacquer & the ballet of brush strokes

Agent Orange left a legacy
in the bodies of a generation

beauty growing out of the bay

the night folds itself around us
water, rock & sky
a little rain drips a fishing boat sets a ripple
a wake of freedom
achingly more beautiful
as arms have drawn life into the world
as hands have held this universe
& wrapped it in a swaddling of sky

dawn breaks light wraps rocks
growing out of the bay
stars sit a few feet above our heads

this is where dreams swim

on   mirror street
on knife street
on art street
all labour is a noun

in the humid patience
the hammock sway afternoon
fish grow bigger for the evening's menu

my daughters shop for hours
in the Old Quarter
& sleep late exhausted
behind the hotel's window

white hand washed
shirts of children
line up in the dust
the school bus is thirty minutes late

waiting for my daughters
exhausted across king-sized beds
in three star hotels

in the quiet of the broken generator
small children twist
in their new school uniforms

a child's birthday wrapped and nourished

yellow star on red is the sun

along the foreshore
old men rub the age
they have become

the boys draw their boxed nets
catching the morning
a labour of folding perfect squares
fish flap around their feet

heat strings through the radiator bars
for the day to explode

at the grocery a few miles of condoms
spool across the counter

you have tucked the hem of the night
into your knickers & crossed your legs

flat warm Tiger Beer

a coconut grove strung like poles
along the esplanade to hold up the sky

church grey granite more European
at this latitude a lasso of colonisation

it is more my astonishment
while watching television
in an internet café in Northern Cambodia
when Hung Seng appears
& the young woman
behind the counter is surprised
when I name him
as the current Prime Minister
who three days ago
scraped through in an election
& is now setting about
maintaining a majority by horse trading
with the minor parties
that she undercharged me
for a couple of emails home
to Kevin Rudd

Nha Trang beach littered
with stars & stripes
reading *The Quiet American*

I open the sweet
potato grilled

to black char
wrapped

in *English
Language Test 4*

*for Form 6*
the outside skin

comes off easily
the flesh

inside is hot
& doughy

&, *I give you peace*
she may have said

holding both my hands in hers
at the 6 o'clock Mass

St Joseph Cathedral
Hanoi, one Thursday

later while walking
back to the hotel

a parishioner said
*I saw you*

*accept the Eucharist*
*I have a friend in Sydney*

*who is a priest*
*do you know him?*

on the roof garden flowers
bloom under a midday sun

& this morning
the young man
who had been
mugged the night before
was tearing up
paper taken from his wallet
it was not an old love letter

the tinkering of iceblocks
a comfort of humidity
thick air sandwich

birdcage early morning

the urban ballet
a few cigarettes & iceblock black coffee
a sculpture of fruit markets
straw broom scrape
in the rush hour horn toot of motorbikes

mid-afternoon thunderclap
drumbeat pause
& then the rain

a blind man arm in arm
with an elderly woman
shuffle along the footpath
in her hand is a bundle of lottery tickets
for the late afternoon draw
in one of his nostrils is a flute
in the other is something like an earplug
his fingers tap out a tune
in the woman's other hand is a plastic bag
which opens in the sway of their walking
they pass by me
when a young man
in a security uniform
takes a handful of tickets
& after some examination selects one
or two and hands the rest back
with some money & waits for the woman
to count out the change
from the plastic bag
they return to me
she holds out the remaining tickets

a young department store
security officer
harasses a Buddhist nun
his uniform looks very new

children rest in our laps
their legs spotted with the scars of old sores

their bodies are washed
& then passed on

drip drying over the open drains
under the veranda's sanctuary

a mild chaos of the day

we swing the children into the air
on a line of grace
in the thick fanned afternoon

a breath would draw us into the new light
in the curtain waving afternoon children sleep on floors
their bodies stuck cold & fed

sharing the school desk our knees knock
a grammar of rules half remembered

*it is time to be tranquil*

ravishing towards sleep

in the afternoon
a regular thud of balls
bounce in the shade

her face is all eyes staring

the lazy eating walk in the shade Sunday

there was this one time
when it all made sense
a spoon, a bowl & a child

a new language soft & uncertain

in the afternoon wet
a river off the awnings
an ocean appears on the road
& the town floats away

the day begins with the opening giggle

toddlers around my legs
a baby in my arms

the back beach elbows itself into the South China Sea
punches above its weight

row upon row crabs shells stacked
a tower of beer cans it must be Sunday

packing up in the wind off the balcony
a rattling of tin, roof flutter, a bird's wing unfolds

a slow brush of wind
against our prickly heat bodies
resting in the arms of each other

in the birdsong morning
caged in the rising light

in the dazing half-eyed afternoon
dreaming of rain

the Old Quarter's clutter

thirty-cent beers in cold-water-rinsed glasses

the rise & fall of morning prayers

& only the brave
or the dumb
or the insured dance in the traffic

the rubbish piles uncollected

reading Charles Bukowski's
*Slouching Towards Nirvana*
in a Hanoi bookshop
the old fuck
would have appreciated
the irony

Mass & the gripping of hands
*Peace be with you*

the dampness
a little wind
to flap out the balcony's washing
over Hang Trong Street

under the overcast sky
hanging heavy
a wedding reception is prepared

the glitz street bristles
inside Crazy Kim Bar
an English lesson begins

a couple of blocks
bar stacked & patient
the sun has slipped into a cocktail glass
the mass of wet bodies giggling the day awake

these are the slow
afternoons fluttering
the world at the end of the day

the long elbow beach
laid out broad as a smile

the sun on my belly cat warmed reading

to sleep in the soft white dawn

a whisper of a dream

*You have to mistrust statues*

in the afternoon city heat
rush hour avoid the footpath
a cigarette butt thrown in a perfect arc

stacked like bricks end on end
these plaited homes
mid-afternoon thunderstorm

too old for the main event

here the shop is God

the airy swing of a Beer Chang bottle
backpacker romanticism

an old man limping down superhighways

patience grows like rot

the mountains hang dense & thick
green fruit balances in bowls
on the table's plain

those tough old uneven pavements
of no straight answers

reptilian faces, arms draped
over a young woman's shoulder

I'm wearing my teeth on my sleeve
in my pocket

if we have picked over the bones
who will come next

*I want a life. I want a home. I want to fall in love, to drink a beer in public. I want to walk in the sunshine and in the rain and see my mother without fear. I want to laugh and not talk about myself as if I were a patient with a terminal disease*

cold teak underfoot

*Never walk in front of a blind elephant*

smoking on the pavements rattling the day

a man is curled asleep outside the roller coaster shut bar
someone has reheated last night's food
& left it for his breakfast snoring steam

a wind of tailored cotton flutters
gently across her growing belly

a history of its people
a history of a souvenir

driven through the sky

as absent hearts would break from lack of patterns

## sand

The sand between
the toes child

on the beach
maybe two

years old
a handful

of light in
both hands

his back
against the Gulf

he stares long
& hard at his mother

who is Buddha
squat staring back

eye to eye
at the possibilities

## café

Outside the café's billboard
a whiff of homemade

on a thread of air
on a thread of memory

my mother all wool
& stockings & raisin toast

& a son in shorts
a set table of treats

## change

Having twisted
canes around

their wires & tied off
& waited for a little rain

to draw through
barely breathing limbs

for buds, to green to leaf & flutter
as children have run with flags

along wet arteries
bleeding change

**south**

Flat line horizon
at the end of a graze

a floating dream
smoke stacked

& silently sailing south

## hand

The pat down window rattle fear of children
at the end of the day a sense of seed
a cup of earth an opened hand

## **north daughter**

In the dusty
light this flat broad sky

cotton flags of family
gather a lap of bay

a lazy wave
of an arm above

the steering
wheel snake

highway south

waiting tables
backpacker

top end
dreaming

a wait of days
dressing up breakfast

turning down supper

a boardwalk
of stars

the hum of the road
drive by bird chatter

through an egg cracked morning

along these lizard tongues
hedged with palms

a sprawl that can't contain
the wind's rattle

galvanised iron
applause

rock pools
& the rush

of falling
white water

over whiter legs
in the wash

we turn back
onto the highway

drive into the sun
totems of flood markers

flat water
nestled in the bay

rolls of cotton blue
overhead the lazy fan

miles of fly wire
at the other end of country

suburbs of village squares
tropics at the curb

only four wheel drivers
importing dust

the morning simmers
fire will come

out of the sun
overhead fans white tiles a dry air

& somehow light
is in the shade

a tropic of salad
along the roadside
louvered windows to the sky

artefacts of a childhood
tacked to the walls
the albums brick stacked

a sliding door screened
to the outside

daughter turn & grow
towards the light

you have staked
what it is that holds you here

in the absence of television

ragtag of coast
this torn cloth flat & blue thrown

a net to pull its harvest
we balance our feet

tread delicately over
blades of thin rock

## August

& finally
the sun

against
our backs

bent under
buds along

the trellis
& desire

a squint
towards

a glass
horizon

## camel rides

Here is
a story

stretched across
Belgium linen

painted in
French oils

& framed
each finished

piece journalled
to the wall

the flick
card colour

of a history
handed up

& over
red dots

& a grandson
done with

camel rides

**return**

A windmilling
of daughters

through the doorway
bare boards clatter

typewriter racket
lassoing a day

& then another
a family album

snapshots on the run
behind their eyes

# hospice

for Jan

& finally
a breath

& the dimpled
Gulf, a brush

of wind like a kiss
flutters wood

against wooden
blinds knocking

an afternoon's rhythm
as the rest

of the ward sleeps
I feel the pulse

in your hand
in my hand

there is time to sleep
after the cup

of ice chips
have melted

all your words

## between

Here is a line drawn
as if to divide the page

& pose the question
earth or air

where to place the sun
as a man would

place a cross
to mark the spot

& draw back
& king hit

& another man
would fall

on another spot
between earth & air

## bud

Bud burst
green flags

shiver on
the brittleness

of light

**suns**

My father
is still in

the house
he built

with his wife
those hand

held walks
after work

from three suburbs
away, to plant

a garden
as the bricks

became walls
& as the fruit

trees budded
walls became

rooms, became
a life of oranges

as big as suns
heavy & ripe

just touching
an earth

that was forever

## ghosts

& the past
is a ghost

behind your eyes
as we drive

a present
reduced to

familiar utterances
too long

far too long
in the company

of each other
a father in his nineties

& a son skipping into
sixty & still spoiling

adult daughters
a cling wrap of dreams

& shared libraries
& a wife renovating

the twilight
with good taste

& an eye
for the bargain

of longevity

## **wrap**

The bird, maybe
a sparrow

wrapped its claws
around the overhead line

& as kids
we would go inside

the closest house
& turn on a light

& return to the street
electric with excitement

expecting to see
a body of feathers

fall fluttering death
on a street we believed

would last forever

## green

In the slow drag
of the afternoon

my father sits among
the folds of shifting light

as shadows play across
the room he is slowly disappearing into

cat lap curl enough miaow
to raise & gather that which

relies on him
as his garden spreads

across the veranda up & over
the neighbours' fences

turning galvanised iron green

**air**

As coming
up for air

means breath
a break in the water

exploding & then
a mouth drawing

until lungs
rattle & dog shake

ocean around
swelling to a beach

a swim away

## pose

Hands under his armpits
his elbows become wings

as he rocks into the night
a pendulum of spine & rags

my father has taken this pose
& I have also sat like this

in those hunched moments
threads against the cold

against certainty
but this man is not my father

& I am not this man
at the market end of town

between closing & opening
a night on the tiles

he sways & sways again
as a small bird heart would beat

& flutter & flutter again

**away**

Away from
the ward's

grey maybe
twenty turns

of the wheel
chair's roll

you can turn
your face

to the winter's sun
& for a moment

a landscape flutters
& flutters again

behind your
blinking eyes

## shake

I shake
out a father's

clothes soft rags
design new quilt

over an unmade bed
flexed for the living

in the shuffling
piss smell of his age

& having done
what sons do for fathers

& done again
I could sleep again

in this room
my mother's

dressing gown
fifteen years a shadow

hooked behind
the bedroom door

## blue line

Oh this blue line horizon
around the neck
of the world
a beer belly sun dips
& spreads unfastens
& lets go its weight
the day staggers
in comfortable trousers

## for Florence

Your weight
barely dents

the fabric
over your bed

a life of quilts
made simple

& held up
your room

a lighter shade
of more than ninety years

artefacts of grace
taught generation

to generation
to generation

& on your bedside cabinet
the water glass holds autumn

## wishing

In the first
few days of winter

the sun is lollipop
bright stuck

on a stick
of horizon

as if a child
& wishing

could bring
a bigger one

## the father

It was a good
day for your funeral

overcast & damp
I couldn't just

step outside
for cigarette

someone you never
met gave me an A plus

for your eulogy
that's teacher talk

for better than average
you were better than average

most of the time
as in those *moments*

*of infinite grace*
when you ruffled

a cowlick head of childhood

## patterns

& the lawn green
as children once danced a ballet

of sunburn under the fall
from sprinklers

& later filled the bath
to the brim & swam

the length Christmas
& back again

turning like seals
end to end to end

# grief

A wash of Chinese ink
& then an emerald cloud framed
the gallery is perched, the underground rattles
& there is no wait time
as the street sings under the weight of swung bags
late Saturday afternoon Orchard Road
& in the dust of roadworks the footpaths widen for commerce
a mall built around water, beer flows on the plaza

into the bird chatter dawn
kids hold the place to ransom
mobile phones, six shooters to the fluttering trees
I step through wet party town
dodge Christmas decorations
& let the tropic light around me

in one of those nine-hundred-room hotels
east meets west buffet breakfast gluttony
& it really doesn't matter
if the eggs aren't free range
here the staff have done their courses
in the gentle art
to find the newspaper & open the day

into the overcast morning
the fun run has closed the expressway
Changi Airport is a mall before a heaven of clouds
with a smoker's room to die for

outside the departure lounge
the familiar fashion frolic of returning Filipinos

a passenger is kneecapped by the plane's food trolley
limping above the world we close ranks
& are offered too many free drinks

& then a dash across Manila at peak hour
a prayer in patience lost luggage dreaming

through the wash of streets
a rhythm of heat & the pimping of stars
lined up & ragged scripts folded & unfolded
& the creases of beauty harden in the grappling night

Kym from Shalom, the Christian Hostel
drives with poorly bandaged broken knuckles
& tells me he got them fighting
he looks at the splint on my arm
I tell him *from taking on the bad guys*
& he wants to know if I'm a pastor
I think about what I'll say next

we talk the mantra of fathers
our children & their school fees

the first English language lesson on Negros is policy
*who speaks, to whom & on whose authority?*
I reframe it, *winners* & *losers*
& *remember those at the margins*
one of the Year 11s laughs

after school at the Su-ay market
I run into three teachers on their way
to pay their condolences
a student from a few years ago died three days ago
when any young man in his mid-twenties
is driving the family car
numbers & timing are everything
there is no second language for grief

the parish priest rides by on a motor bike
the scramble of pieces that make a pattern
I drink rum close to the shade of a mango tree
waiting for the world to bloom into fruit

the calm dawn dog bark dark
the humidity sets around us
a tablecloth for the morning

when two old men talk over coffee
they rest in their silences
translations of an age

I try to teach metaphor
& retell a story about my parents
*I look in the mirror & my father stares back*

I grab a handful of sugared peanuts & taste candy all day

*Ma'am* closes the school two hours early
the entire staff attends a memorial service for the ex-student
the father, an ex-priest, rages against his God
rattles past the cliché of *potential*
& *the exchange of a life*
this is rock hard no nonsense anger
a young man fragile is that moment
where a rush of blood filled his eyes
& clotted his heart against the order of how he planned to live
& in the rain afterwards
& in the click & flutter of mah-jong tiles & cards
small table stakes & chancers & other entertainments
a family waits & waits to gather to bury him

against a father's chest, a mother's breast
they held & fed you, heart against beating heart
& now the rain has set in, I toast the storm
overflowing the drains which carries a river

we dream into the middle distance
between rain & sun & after the storm
reveal what it is that brought us here
a hand within a hand within a hand
laid to rest gently into this earth

I walk the length of the Barangay
the roosters crow
a small measure of settlement
to loosen our limbs & extend our lives
a greeting with each step
in the sway awake rhythms of each other's lives
as the cock is placed into the ring

the classrooms chant
the heat of the day rises

in the front room of Anawim, centre for the deaf
hands are raised & touched to foreheads & blessed
a gurgling joy as the candy is hidden until after dinner

& I ask about Christopher's welfare
& am told by his father that he has died
but not already dead

we eat bread & drink coffee over the estuary
the mangroves flutter behind us
empty rum bottles hang together on lines
& clink the approach of friend & stranger

after mass for the Feast of the Immaculate Conception
we play *Find Mary* amongst the students
pinning a red petal to their humanity

driving from Su-ay to Bacolod
we pass a man with his arms under his head
his right leg has exploded opening to bone
his motor cycle pushed to the side
the truck that hit him stalled further down the road
two men stand over the body & direct traffic
they are waiting for the police to arrive
& then, maybe then, a cover to reduce our fears
later in the airport's smoking room
I drink Pilsen & smoke enough cigarettes to pollute an island state

we spend an entire day
preparing for the wedding
videoed from every angle
the speeches are still going
as the chairs are packed away
& I take off my *barong*
guard the gifts as the reception is ferried home
in one overflowing single car

we gather in our smiles
at morning tea
the unexplainable is silent
washing over us
a mass is built around a life
this abundance of food
we rest between speakers
as a new world is created in our arms
this commissioning
& afterwards beer, rum & karaoke
it must be Sunday

in the street the labour
of enterprise
each space built upon itself
to profit a life
small money huge effort
to begin each day
& then the rain floods
as the brooms of the Barangay
shift the rubbish
down drains in the dim dawn
we roll & sweat against the moving air
to this resting time

at the parish party a bottle of Jack Daniel's appears
it must be Christmas
*the gift must be long* & I receive two belts

sleep children sleep
there will be a morning at the end of it

## note

& when the breath comes
it comes deep almost gut deep to rattle

& on a note the bass side of a scream
scatters all that heart & earth & ripples

as a gunshot blast would send a cloud
of cockatoos into the sky

**tears**

& when the bar girl recalls you
from a couple of years ago
on the plaza behind Orchard Road
you know there is something in the air
& on the table one sweating Tiger Beer
a bucket of ice & two glasses
*don't complicate it*

The calm humid morning purr of tricycles
a cruise of cabs
smoking just off Pedro Gil Street
Manila Bay over my shoulder
& Robinson's Place white against
the morning's commerce sleeps

The night before we hold hands standing
a grace at the long table of Mr Poon's

A straight-edge hot-towel shave
two brandies later
I can still thread a needle in the half light
& sew a button at any age

The bitumen sings concrete rusts
a bus moans through back streets
I order a thermos of hot water for three in one coffee
& a three in the morning wake-up call

At the Su-ay Market the smile of Angelique
& the sky rains candy
I sit with her sister Rose
in the burnt-out shell of their shop
the day after the fire they cleaned up
the next day was trading as usual
their savings bought new stock
insurance is a first-world luxury

I drink a couple of almost cold beers
delivered tops off from the shop next door

Love is a crucifix around the neck of the day
I buy a dozen at the Columban Mission & get one free

At the afternoon end of the school day calm
I unblock the toilet
the students rehearse the Novena
for tomorrow night's Mass
it's one of those Mary & Martha moments
& I'm up to my elbows in someone's shit

A tree grows out of the school kitchen
chicken curry & rice for ten pesos
that's twenty-five cents
rather than chop it down
the cooks have learnt to walk around its girth

Mangrove planting & the earth rises
a big lunch inside stilted houses
over the estuary fish jump into nets
& the students delight in their easy labour

In the cotton-clad night
a dream of rain to raise the crops from our lives
I sip brandy made from sugar cane
& reread the label too many times

At the dam we strip down to ourselves
& wash away the last few days
it is the Feast of Saint Lorenzo Ruiz
& lunch is spectacular

John Carl brushes his lips against my face
a lit candle & flowers are on the table
his brother dead almost a year & with these new tears
we sip water in the house of his parents
his grandmother wants to feed us

*The bus will be here in five minutes*
we rest in our silences & move through the day
this is a three beer wait
& I'm doing the washing up from lunch
when the driver knocks on the scullery door

A joyful ballet dancing language of the deaf

Here we have unpicked time to let it settle around us
looking for threads to knit a pattern
we hug the coast road to Bacolod

After breakfast we stroll through the Barangay
pick up from where we left off
multiple breakfasts house-warming & flowers

An almost cold beer for morning snack
afternoon tea is coconut wine & chicken & noodles
supper is a feast & kids filling the house

& when the water comes it breaks
the sky open & the street's a flood of litter
& then through the calm
we step around our silences
a prayer to the cooling night
a string of taxis turn to where land ends

## for Reginald Whitely cfc

A baptismal
cloth is placed

over your coffin
white beyond white

beyond metaphor
as a body danced

through a rhythm
of language naming

those not yet born
to be baptised

## against

On this stretch of winter beach
a grey sky drawn to a grey sea

against a grey horizon
a man & a five-year-old

hands grasped against the wind
swing against the wind

& there just before
the breaking of the rain

a rainbow & then another
& another

& he throws the child
into his chest & carries her

their backs against the storm
her first rainbow & there were three

## take

We take
our wait

resting in
the white

hospitalised
age of who we are

we are there
in a grace

a here & a now
but listen

for the breath
& then another

& then we know
we are alive

breathe the now
a hand on your heart

breathe again

## cloak

A cloak
of cloud

over our
shoulders

horizons
a gaze away

these patterns
long-lived prayers

as days drip
a cupping

of hands
& on the beach

a sand castle
from the day

before almost
holds the tide

## junk

Day slip
hospital green

a passage through
the red of your blood

& the tests
vials one hand

juggling
a crease of arm

which you open
almost as junk

would take a life
& you want to live

**story**

Thrown down & then a random
settling to toe poke a pattern

& make some sense from this distance
as if memory caught could now

order the photographs
by date, place & who

your death notice
is about as solid as it gets

## daughter, Chinatown

& on the street she twirled
her skirt circled up around

a carousal of blue
& white until enough

& then a dizziness
of pause as the fabric

fell & rested below
her knees & she returned

just in time for dessert
one Chinese New Year

many years ago
when the lion visited

& the restaurant
received its blessing

& good fortune

**body**

Your blood cells
are at war with themselves

confusing the order of living
how in the not so long ago

daughters clung to your limbs
& you wrapped them

a tendril of arms
heart against beating heart

healing & inhaling
their downy heads

**roots**

After their deaths
we spread the elements

dig them down to strike
in the loamy dampness

of ourselves & then hand
on to granddaughters

the new beginnings
a bud burst of colour

in jam jar vases lining a windowsill
& watch the roots expand

& float as air would fill lungs
a doctor's certain tap on your back

## reach

for Brother Gerald Faulkner cfc

Here is the reach
of your voice

past naming
where sky

meets ocean
& further still

where you imagined
the unimaginable

on your lips your song
for the new world's harmony

## Mila

It is the shadow of you
where you slept soundly

the mattress on the floor
a sleeping bag cocoon

pulled to your eyes
with enough emptiness

to form & grow the shape of you
from where you burst through

& out of in first light
your visiting is recorded in songs

sung in the spaces of your future

## **ward**

The day after Easter the cancer ward
is packed cigarette-tight

we walk, as a couple
arms through each other
as if a long marriage would challenge intimacy

the volunteers are open & chatty
every patient with a head scarf
is spoken to, almost levity

the lack of magazines
means bring a novel
*the thousand yard stare*

empathy rides a dark horse
where you are in treatment
& where treatment is in you

this is not a fashion show
style never left home
even the young wear comfortable shoes
there is always diversity
Medicare card & a light bag
a change of clothes in the car

a hospital packed case
is a phone call away
they all know the drill

there are rivers here
& the walk is bare foot
over pebbles along its edge

the business edge of the care industry
ends in a variety of tears
& when the fires burns

it unbuttons a nakedness
a broken language
our elbows touch each other

## before

for Pam Kelly

Before your interment took place
I left the memorial & at home

dug deep into the garden
stacking bricks to retain

what was left of the beds
to hold back the fall of earth & keep

what was planted growing
later spacing out cuttings of geranium

& the rootstock of mother-in-law's tongue
in the dampness the season gave

of purpose, labour, grief & time

## pier

The wind in the sails of ourselves
a billow of shirt as if three sheets

we bend into its embrace
a sand print at a time

the pier of you
is an arm length away

# milk

for Roger

We are here in the south
while your son of almost sixty-six
is being buried in the west
& the time difference
of your ninety-sixth years
means when I leave
you will be sent a recording of his memorial
you old time Methodist
both temperance & aspiration
who nursed me
a few weeks after my birth
while my mother haemorrhaged
so dramatically that 1950s medicine
& a father on the line
meant an early change to formula
& a three-hour train ride
to a town smelting lead
but now on this gathering day
around a table hallmarked sympathy
we simply sit with an uncertain rage
against the natural order of things

## old roads

A week before spring
& maybe twenty klicks
from my grandparents graves
I turn through this unsealed randomness
& breathe the late winter runoff
green ravines & scrub
I was too lazy to name or learn properly
if not childhood, then what
years of wandering Kuitpo Forest
under canvas & a mischief
of a past that we survived
& this big sky country
of finding a way out to home
right now it seems right
road, verge, a landscape beyond
& the promise of direction
old roads to drive like signs glimpsed at
gathering pine cones to begin the day

## shape

& we spread
the blanket

around your form
fold in the edges

& tuck deep
around the shape

of you to hold
a dreaming

& then stand back
& watch, & simply watch

## cold

& the cold dog bite
an hour or so before the sun

massages the earth
I run in the dark under stars of ice

A shuffle of dripping streets
neons explode like stars

a brittleness of bobbing heads
wool-wrapped shoulders

feet dance to keep warm
& quicken their pace

towards mango dreaming
small gulps of dark rum

dark wide beach stretch
I stub my toe on a grain of sand

## wait

In the wait
we have

held a universe
of children close

to ourselves
& now this

the exchange
if not a life

then something
that has filled

an address with
song & things

to gift the living

## blue

The wind
in my ears

the cat
has finally

come in
& my wife

blank with
the vagueness

of chemotherapy
lies under

a white sheet
in a hospital

bed breathing
at the end

of a big
blue sky day

## **steam**

You are able
to bathe

yourself
leaning forward

sculptured
from the shower chair

the jets of water
run rain warm

over the pink skin
topography

of your body
until you have

grown impatient
enough of that moment

& then the measured
progress of patting you dry

the IV line in your arm
glad wrap

& you rise as a mother
would to greet

a child at her knees
& I bend your arms

dressing oh so gently
through fresh blue cotton

in the steam-teared
bathroom of ward 7E

**view**

At thirty-five thousand feet
even the good country
is snakes & ladders

# Dorset suite

for Jim & Anna


Cock & hen walls around the town, the wet
green shimmer dawn clings
as a hand to a face
the cold wash under the sky

Old stuff, big houses
the lanes that wind
& blow history forwards on a string

Tom Roberts was born here
a lack of graffiti
no tags & no ink
a conservative landscape of Tory voters
with their children on school holiday

In the longer term before them
their feet rattle the footpaths
bodies wool & puffer cling
a rustling of plastic overcoats

An absent rhythm of school bags
bumping on their backs
right now it is freedom

From the colonies to this grace of generosity

Rock into rock the great shifts
as earth planes & shaves
& rumbles & planes & shaves
its guts as it shears to the sea
across the water is France

The green is thrown up everywhere
through the gaps in village thatch
& the winding of roads like springs

On Shrove Tuesday
I walk the wet edges of fields
the motorway over my shoulder
a scarf & a steady step through mud
dog bark & wet weather gear every shade of rural green

The rise & fall of limbs
over a farmer's land
a smear of black across foreheads

Collars tucked wet necks
a few days before spring
the sky a black tea stew

A bite of wind pink flushed
damp backs from the way we came
boots draw water from the turf
of turf to where we will return

& the gutters run all day
rain beat our collars damp
even the birds are hiding

Portland stone unforgiving as a prison town

During mass our coats steam

The high street's puddles cobble a river

Trouser ends fray damp around the ankles
grass seeds germinate in wet cuffs

The sign of peace
one hand still in our dripping coats

& yes the prognosis
for a long life is not good
as if a series of numbers
could determine what it is to live towards
behind double-glazed doors Dorchester

In a narrow back garden
a wait for a bud burst of time
that the spring calendar has promised
there are no printed certainties
except the pencilled staggered opening times
of four or five pubs within walking distance

You hug this rugged coastline
as if your life depended on it & it does

When the rain stops
we will dress ourselves for the walk into town
for the warm rush of pints
& leave wet socks on the radiator bars of central heating

## & now

& now
the Earth

has pulled
back, enough

is enough
rolled up

its sleeves
backed itself

against itself
to hold off

what it is
we most fear

ourselves

## there

Live in it
& breathe

this moment
as a grace

would settle
over us

as a cloud
would part

& there
is the light

a sun

## wide

The wide
canvas is blank

my wife has died
her absence is profound

as in those moments
when I expect to hear

a voice & delegation
of a long marriage

the cat, the well fed cat
sleeps in the back room

on my absent parents' chairs
we have collected

too much
in this short life

## touch

The hesitant
touch from you

as a breeze
would disturb

the order
of ourselves

& leave a ruin
we stretch

towards light
recovering

piece by piece
in the shadow

always in the shadow
from where we came

to where we are going

## cemetery

The broken
bits of graves

I walk between
as memory

would somehow
dig deep this absence

& then a few
bunches of flowers

to repair a history
of this, ourselves

& others into the deep
which we stare into

dark & damp
& uncertain

the sky above us

## caught

We open
our eyes

to this
a fog of

ourselves
the roads

we walk
along this winter

the sun
has been

caught, a ball
thrown to

the extremes
of who we are

one bounce
& then another

to the far
reach of

of being
caught

& held
& cherished

as a child
would be

captured
& nourished

& loved
& gently

lowered, blanket
wrapped to sleep

## slide

Let it slide
just a little

some domestic
upheaval

a death maybe
or a blocked drain

as we rush
towards the heart

of ourselves
& call it grace

or a missed
opportunity

there is a child
waiting for birth

just wait
& breathe

# Acknowledgements

ABC Radio Adelaide, *Beer Swill Romanticism*,
*English in Australia, Eureka Street, Famous Reporter, fourW,
Friendly Street Readers, InDaily, Insight, Mekong Review,
Omega, Polestar Writers' Journal, Purple &White 2020, Studio,
The Canberra Times, _ this breath is not mine to keep,
Unusual Work*

Roberto Saviano
Graham Rowlands
Claire Woods

From the late 1970s, the author received funding from the Literature Board of the Australia Council for poet-in-residences in local and country schools. He toured with the Australian Performing Group's Poetry Workshop through Victoria (1979). He received funding from the Australian Schools Commission, Carclew, Department of Education South Australia, and Arts SA for various projects including year-long poet-in-residencies at Woodville HS (1981) and Elizabeth West Schools (1983). He co-wrote with Peter McFarlane a series of poetry textbooks for the Australian Association for the Teaching of English and Macmillan Education Australia. His radio dramas have been broadcast on National Radio Solomon Islands. He currently teaches at Playford College, South Australia.

www.ingramcontent.com/pod-product-compliance
Lightning Source LLC
Chambersburg PA
CBHW050250120526
44590CB00016B/2286